The Ohio Lands
Photography *of* Ian Adams
Text *by* John Fleischman

THE OHIO LANDS

PHOTOGRAPHY *of* IAN ADAMS
TEXT *by* JOHN FLEISCHMAN

BROWNTROUT PUBLISHERS, INC.
SAN FRANCISCO

THE OHIO LANDS
Photography by Ian Adams
Text by John Fleischmann

(Preceding Pages)

Snow covers dune grasses at Mentor Headlands State Nature Preserve in Lake County. This 16-acre area is one of a handful of natural beaches remaining along Lake Erie's heavily-developed south shore. Monarch butterflies and migrating birds rest here, at the northern terminus of the 1200-mile Buckeye hiking trail.

Ludlow Falls is the largest of several waterfalls along Ludlow Creek in southwestern Ohio's Miami County. Glacial action and stream erosion have carved potholes, cliffs, and cascades along Ludlow Creek, Greenville Creek, and other tributaries of the Stillwater River, one of Ohio's ten state scenic rivers.

Library of Congress Cataloging-in-Publication Data

Adams, Ian J.
    The Ohio lands / photography of Ian Adams : text by John Fleischman.
        p.   cm.
    ISBN 1-56313-739-9 (alk. paper)
    1. Ohio—Pictorial works. I. Fleischman, John.   II. Title.
    F492.A62   1995   95-24974
    977.1'0022'2—dc20   CIP

                10 9 8 7 6 5 4 3 2 1
        Published in the United States of America by
                BrownTrout Publishers, Inc.
                P.O. Box 280070
                San Francisco, California 94128

        Set in type by Top Hat Typography, San Mateo
        Printed and bound by Everbest, Hong Kong

DEDICATION
This book is dedicated to the many organizations and individuals who are working
to preserve Ohio's natural and historical heritage.

Mallards go ice skating near a causeway at Cedar Point near Sandusky.
Other species often seen in large flocks in late winter include greater and lesser scaups,
canvasbacks, redheads, oldsquaws, and mergansers.

FROM THE PHOTOGRAPHER

I am often surprised at how unaware many native Ohioans seem to be about the natural and historical heritage of their state. Perhaps this book will foster a better awareness of Ohio's many wonders. To those who know the state well, I hope the book will recall memories of pleasant times spent in favorite Buckeye places, and perhaps reveal a few new ones as well. To those who have yet to discover Ohio's special places, I hope that the book will open their eyes to the beauty and fascinating history of this wonderful state.

ABOUT THE PHOTOGRAPHY

The scenic photographs in the book were made primarily with a Sinar F 4x5-inch view camera, using lenses from 75mm to 360mm, and a Fuji GX680 6x8cm camera, using lenses from 65mm to 250mm. Nikon F3 cameras, with lenses from 24mm to 600mm, were used for wildlife and close-up subjects. A tripod was used for all photographs, and a polarizing filter was used, albeit sparingly, to intensify colors and reduce specular reflections. Large- and medium-format images were made using Fujichrome 50 (RFP), Velvia (RVP), and Fujichrome 100 (RDP) films. Kodachrome 25 and 64 films were used for some of the 35mm images.

ACKNOWLEDGEMENTS

First and foremost, I would like to thank Marc and Wendover Brown of BrownTrout Publishers for undertaking this book as part of BrownTrout's book publishing program. Our collaboration during the past eight years of "Wild & Scenic Ohio" and "Ohio Places" calendars has been a true pleasure as well as a critical part of my photography career.

I would like to acknowledge fellow Ohio photographer Gary Meszaros, who introduced me to many of Ohio's flora, fauna, and natural areas, and helped refine my photographer's eye and field skills.

Guy Denny of the Ohio Department of Natural Resources, Division of Natural Areas and Preserves shared his encyclopedic knowledge of Ohio's State Nature Preserves and provided access permits, help, and encouragement. Guy and his staff also gave freely of their time to proof the captions and make needed corrections. The Ohio Chapter of The Nature Conservancy provided access to many of their Ohio preserves.

Since 1988, many of my Ohio photographs have been published in a variety of articles in *Ohio* Magazine, which has been chronicling the Ohio scene for more than 17 years. Special thanks to John Baskin, Ellen Stein Burbach, John Fleischman, Sue Gorisek, and Brooke Wenstrup for their encouragement, support, and friendship throughout my Ohio photography endeavors.

My thanks to Akron Commercial Color Lab and Quick Photo in Akron for their high-quality processing of my color film, and to the staff of KD Color in Cleveland for their expert work in producing Ilfochrome (Cibachrome) color prints from many of my photographs.

Many other good friends provided help and advice, pleasant company, a good meal, or a place to stay at the end of a long day in the field. I would especially like to thank Diane Chalfant, Dennis Conley, Bruce and Yvonne Cubberley, Kathy Dlabick, David and Nancy Dvorak, Judie Gauss, Joe Jesensky, Jennie Jones, Bill Kibler, David Kline, Arthur and Florence Koenig, Brenda Lewison, Kathy McGee, John and Beth Marshall, Ray Novotny, Kevin O'Neil, Marilyn Ortt, John Randolph, Jim Roetzel, Karl Smith, Bert Szabo, and Rick Zaidan.

Finally, I would like to thank my parents, Margie and Tony McCarthy, who provided frequent encouragement and support during my transition from a career in corporate information systems to freelance environmental photography.

CONTENTS

INTRODUCTION – COMING INTO THE OHIO COUNTRY   11

1   A WALK IN THE WOODS   16

2   IN WET PLACES   30

3   GREAT LAKE EFFECTS   44

4   RIVERLANDS   56

5   THE GREAT PLAIN   70

6   HILLS AND HOLLOWS   82

7   GOING TO THE COUNTRY   94

8   GOING TO TOWN   108

9   INTO THE GARDEN   120

10   THE FOUR SEASONS, AN OHIO PHOTOGRAPHIC SUITE   132

Royal catchfly, wild bergamot, and gray-headed coneflower bloom at Bigelow Cemetery Prairie State Nature Preserve in Madison County in west-central Ohio. This 1/2-acre pioneer cemetery preserve is a tiny remnant of the tallgrass prairies which once covered this area, known as the Darby Plains.

Deep Lock, or Lock 28, is the tallest of the 44 locks which lowered the old Ohio & Erie Canal more than 300 feet from Summit Lake at Akron to Lake Erie at Cleveland. Nearby is Deep Lock Quarry, where native sandstone was quarried to build the locks.

(Following Page)

Sunrise pierces morning mist at Clendening Lake in Harrison County. Clendening is one of 14 lakes in eastern Ohio built for flood control, water conservation, and recreation by the U.S. Army Corps of Engineers during the 1930s.

INTRODUCTION
COMING INTO THE OHIO COUNTRY

His Majesty was graciously pleased to signify his royal approbation of Colonel Bouquet's conduct. Having thrashed the savages in battle, the colonel was directed in the autumn of 1764 to advance beyond the forks of the Ohio, taking detachments of the 42nd and 60th regiments of foot along with various Virginia and Pennsylvania colonial volunteers, and there to treat with the defeated tribes. The colonel moved cautiously into the wilderness. Henry Bouquet was Swiss by birth and a mercenary by occupation who'd learned his trade in the service of the King of Sardinia, the Prince of Orange and the Duke of Cumberland. On this bloody western edge of His Majesty's North American territory, Bouquet advanced with skirmishers well forward, his redcoats marching in square and his baggage train close under the eye of his light horse. The broken tribes fled before him.

Bouquet's troops left Fort Pitt on October 4th, following the Ohio River until they reached the mouth of the Little Beaver from where they pressed westward through thick forest into what is now the state of Ohio. His men waded fast, clear-running streams and passed through an "abundance of tall timber." Despite the noise of the advancing army, Bouquet's hunters found ample game for each evening's fortified camp. On October 12th, the expedition's journal reported crossing a branch of the Muskingum River. "Keeping the aforesaid creek on their left, they marched through much fine land, watered with small river and springs; proceeded likewise through several savannas or cleared spots, which are by nature extremely beautiful." The clearings were beautiful to the soldiers because they were a relief from the fathomless forest and the threat of ambush.

To modern eyes, all of it—ancient forest and sudden clearings—seems a paradise lost. When we read the campaign reports and the pioneer journals of those who followed Colonel Bouquet, we glimpse a land of unimaginable natural wealth. "Yesterday, June 18, 1817, I measured a walnut almost seven feet in diameter," Norris Birbank noted in his diary, "clean and straight as an arrow. The white oak is the glory of the upland forest. I measured a white oak

A dogwood flowers near a pond at Spring Grove Cemetery in Cincinnati. Covering 733 acres of wooded hillside, Spring Grove is the largest private nonprofit cemetery in the United States, and has been designated a National Historic Landmark.

by the roadside which at four feet from the ground was six feet in diameter, and at seventy-five feet is measured nine feet around. Before we entered on the flat country were some hills (near Chillicothe) covered with the grandest white oak, I suppose, in America. They measured fourteen and fifteen feet in circumference, their straight stems rising without a branch to seventy-five or eighty feet—thousands of them."

Thousands of them, we marvel. Birbank's giant white oaks were but a few sticks in the great forest that covered the Ohio lands. When the settlers first crossed the Appalachian Mountains in large numbers at the end of the eighteenth century, the state-to-become-Ohio was 95 percent forest, covered in 25 million acres of primeval forest. It was the heart of a once even greater forest. On the October morning in 1492 when Columbus dropped anchor in the Caribbean, that vaster forest all but covered eastern North America from the Gulf Coast to the Canadian tundra, from the Atlantic Ocean to central Minnesota. On a continental scale, it was cut by the western prairies, the Okefenoke Swamp and the Mississippi delta. On a local scale, there were barrens, bogs, grasslands, rocky uplands, tornado tracks, firelands and dunes. Within the forest were natural subdivisions. Between the Southern pinelands and the Northern evergreen tracts was a heartland hardwood forest. Ohio was at the heart of this grand forest.

"The American hardwood forest of history," writer Rutherford Platt called it, "the domain of the woodland Indians, the forest which was so dangerous and unlivable in the eyes of the first English settlers and which we call primeval today, was in truth a luminous, youthful, supple forest, newborn out of the Ice Age. In the nobility and quality of its trees, in the number of species of trees, bushes, vines and flowers; in the purity of lakes and streams, in the abundance and color of its birds and fish and in the personalities of its animals, no other forest that ever grew on earth could be compared with it."

And it was nearly all to go in Ohio. We goggle over the tales of early travelers who walked all day under its canopy, glimpsing the sky only in patches.

Yet the pioneers themselves chiefly remembered a fear of the woods beyond the danger of Indians or wild animals—a dread that they would suffocate under the endless shade. The pioneers were not blind to the breathtaking richness of the Ohio lands but also they measured the back-breaking labor ahead of them to reshape this inhospitable ecology to open field agriculture. Trees were the enemy of farmers who would starve if they could not open corn fields to the sun. The land had to be "claimed," altered for farming, cleared for towns and rechanneled for industry. And, by and large, it was.

Lincoln said that at fifty, a man gets the face he deserves. Whether Ohio, approaching her 200th birthday as a state, has the face she deserves is another question. Certainly Ohio is no longer renowned for wildness or great natural splendor. Yet broad impressions can be misleading. All too often travelers draw their impressions at 65 m.p.h. from an interstate highway or at 600 m.p.h. from 30,000 feet. The checkerboard landscape of modern Ohio that runs past their windows is a blur of fields, towns and roads. And it is misleading. To go slowly and up close in Ohio is to see surprising things. The object of this book is to do just that.

Consider this an invitation to join an expedition by camera into what photographer Ian Adams calls the "Ohio lands." The plural is deliberate. For Ian Adams, the "Ohio lands"—the territory west of the Appalachians, north of the Ohio River and south of Lake Erie—encompass a vast variety of landscapes and ecologies. Some are natural, some manmade. Their roots are ancient and modern, created by forces as great as continental glaciers or as small as a tiny rivulet rising through a shady outcrop of limestone. Geology, geography, weather, plants and creatures especially the human kind have all plied their handiwork here. The Ohio lands are well worth the visit.

Unlike Colonel Bouquet, you will not need to guard your baggage train on this expedition but you should leave behind certain misconceptions about the landscape of the American Midwest. The first piece of mental baggage to go should be the pernicious notion that humans are somehow separate from

A fresh snowfall covers fallen trees in Clear Fork Gorge, part of Mohican State Park in Richland County. Created by stream reversal some 15,000 years ago, Clear Fork Gorge is Ohio's deepest canyon. Several hiking trails lead to scenic overlooks, waterfalls, and rugged sandstone outcrops.

nature. If it's any comfort, this Nature-Apart-From-People idea was an early product of the Ohio frontier; it was a conceit of the settlers that the territory they were occupying was empty. "Virgin forest," they called it, meaning untouched by Man. It manifestly was not.

People have been shaping the Ohio lands for at least 12,000 years. The people we know only as "Paleo-Indians" were the first and only humans to see the Ohio country as truly "virgin"—that is, unpeopled—land. The Paleo-Indians edged in as the last Ice Age drew back, uncovering a marshy land of evergreens and birches, inhabited by spectacular large animals such as the mammoth and the giant sloth. The disappearance of the North American "megamammals" coincides with the appearance of the Paleo-Indians who carried spears topped with razor-sharp flints. Whether the first hunters single-handedly caused the megamammal extinction or not, they began the long human impact on Ohio.

The Indian peoples were not environmental plaster saints, "eco-fairies" living on the land but never altering it. They were human with all the human needs for food, shelter and folly. They were voracious consumers of firewood. During hunts, they set fire to the prairies in western Ohio. They practiced slash and burn agriculture along river bottoms so that when General Anthony Wayne led his conquering army into northwest Ohio in 1794, he marveled at the miles of cornfields along the rivers. He also burned them, which did more than all the shooting battles put together to drive off the tribal farmers.

Even by the most generous estimates, the population at any one time of prehistoric and historic Indians was but a fraction of the white population that flooded into Ohio after 1800. Moreover, Indian technology was limited. They also moved about in the land, following seasonal supplies of food and thus spreading their impact. The American settlers marked the previously "empty" territory into private holdings and stayed in one place, digging in. But Nature doesn't end with the coming of Mad Anthony Wayne.

Nature works around Man, even heroic men like pioneers. In an epic feat of manual labor, Ohio went from 95 percent forest in 1800 to about 15 percent forest around the time of the First World War, almost all of it second growth. In this century, the landscape has changed yet again, allowed to "go back" to wild in some areas and tortured into new developments elsewhere. Ohio is now about 27 percent wooded although the population has never been larger, more spread out and more motorized.

Yet the Ohio lands retain much of their older character. It's easiest to see in "natural" areas of forest, wetland and lake. In Ohio, you can still walk in deep woods of oak, beech, walnut and maple, unseen anywhere else on earth but the American Midwest. You can read the clear traces of glaciation on a land still dotted with kettle lakes and bogs. You can see the patterns of rivers and lakes that steered American history westward. You can explore quiet places and see wonders of flora, fauna and fungi.

A central objective of this photographic foray is to seek out the remnants of the pre-settlement Ohio "biomes," patches of the old ecological provinces of forest, prairie, swamp, marsh, bog, fen, lakeshore and riverlands. All have been altered. Some have nearly vanished but for those who know where to look, the Ohio lands are still rich and unexpected country.

One of the most startling remnants (and the rarest) is the Ohio prairie land. In a country of seemingly endless forest, the great, open meadows of west-central Ohio were a delight to the frontier scouts who followed the Big and Little Darby creeks west into wide grasslands. A man on horseback, they reported, could ride in mid-summer across the Darby Plains, his head and shoulders barely above the waving grasses and blazing wild flowers.

Spring foliage frames a view of the Water Tower in Eden Park, a Cincinnati suburb. Designed by the Hannaford firm to resemble a castle keep, the 172-foot tower, built in 1894, is a favorite city landmark.

These were not the edge of the horizon-to-horizon prairies of the Great Plains but localized tallgrass meadows. Edgar Transeau, the turn-of-the-century Ohio State University ecologist who studied the Darby Plains described them as a "prairie archipelago," grassy islands in an Ohio "ocean" of hardwood forest.

The Ohio prairies proved to be treacherous lands for settlement, poorly drained and armored with thick tallgrass sod that clung tenaciously to the heavy, black soil. In winter, water stood on the surface; malaria was endemic. In summer, galloping grass fires roared across the land, driving terrified animals

and hapless men before them. The Darby Plains remained nearly unsettled until after the War of 1812 when waves of American refugees driven from southern Canada arrived in Ohio, broke and desperate enough to try their luck on prairie land.

It started killing them even before the settlers had the ground surveyed. Hastily buried in impromptu cemeteries, the dead had freehold on the Darby Plains a year before anyone alive could register a claim. Ironically, the pioneer cemeteries became islands within islands, the only patches of prairie never put to the plow as Progress finally bulled its way through the Darby, draining the water and busting the sod.

But before the final destruction, there was a moment to see the Ohio prairie land in its power. "It was, indeed, a grand sight to the nature-loving mind," wrote Jeremiah Converse, an early arrival who practiced medicine on the Darby Plains, "to look over these extensive prairie fields and behold them mantled with so luxuriant a growth of vegetation, and decorated so lavishly with an almost endless variety of flowers, variegated with all the colors of the rainbow, and so blended in beauty that the inmost soul would almost involuntarily praise God for the grandeur of His omnipotent wisdom and power; but to that class of persons who cannot appreciate any loveliness or beauty in the works of nature, it might appear as a God-forsaken wilderness and not intended as a home for civilized humanity."

For the class of persons who want to see the Ohio prairie today, only amongst the weather-bleached headstones of pioneer cemeteries will they find the distinctive prairie grass and forbs—big bluestem, purple coneflower, stiff goldenrod, whorled rosinweed, flowering spurge, sainfoin and the rare royal catchfly. Beyond the fence line, they will look out over some of the richest farmland in America, a drained and tidy landscape of soy beans and corn as far as the eye can see. But they should look down at the plants underfoot. In these old prairie burial grounds and along early railroad lines where spark-spouting locomotives torched the rights-of-way, the true Ohio prairie native species have held out. In recent years, botanists have brought the cleansing fire back into old prairie habitats and painstakingly gathered some of this native stock to reseed or sow from scratch "reconstructed" prairies elsewhere. Humans keep tinkering with the Ohio lands but where we allow an opening, the native ecology reasserts its sovereignty.

If this expedition takes you to some of Ohio's hardiest remnant ecologies, we also propose to open your eyes to certain manmade landscapes distinctive to Ohio. One is a landscape so familiar, it takes a moment to realize that it is both old, endangered and "natural" to a way of life. We mean the nineteenth century Ohio landscape of family farms and small towns. It is a landscape deeply embedded in the American mind as a national memory from a simpler age. Whether your grand or great-grand or great-great-parents actually grew up in such a rural setting, it lingers in American memory. Here families were self-reliant, requiring all able hands to turn to chores, to plowing and harvesting, to farmhouse crafts and animal care. This way of life shaped a landscape which still can be seen in Ohio.

Its greatest preservers are the Amish, a people whose faith and lifestyle is shaped by a galaxy of tiny, independent Anabaptist churches. The Amish community in Ohio is far larger than that of the more publicized "Pennsylvania Dutch" and maintains the traditional rural landscape by carefully defining their technology and their family roles. The Amish farm with draft horses, using traditional farm machinery, manure and few chemicals. A family works no more land than a man, wife and children can manage. It is a self-sustained agriculture that respects both land and human needs. There is, however, a great danger of enveloping the Amish in sentimentality. The photographs here presented looking past the quaint Amish clothes and buggies to see how the Amish preserve this traditional rural Ohio landscape.

Beyond the Ohio family farm was the "county" town, the local center for buying and borrowing with a courthouse for law and the railroad for shipping. It's another American archetype that's under assault from a changing economy and changing technology. The traditional Ohio town landscape is still to be seen for those who will look to the remaining wealth of town architecture—

The Carpenter's Shop is tucked away on a side street at Zoar in Tuscarawas County. A couple of years after the village was established in 1817, the Zoarites abandoned personal property ownership in favor of a communal system. After its leader, Joseph Baumeler, died in 1853, the village began a slow decline until its eventual 1898 dissolution.

wedding cake Victorian courthouses and somber turn-of-the-century mercantile buildings. Even the pattern of their streets reflects a deeply American sense of townscape; new towns in far flung Arizona or California sprouted Maple, Main and Vine streets in memorial. So we look to the towns for another example of the Ohio lands.

There are other native Ohio terrains to be explore here: the wide plain that fronts on Lake Erie; the marshes along the lake edges; the valleys of the Ohio River's great tributaries; the hill country of southeastern Ohio where the last glacier stopped short and left the bones of the land exposed. We will visit these and other lands, some wilder and others more tame.

This photographic expedition dwells on the best of the Ohio landscape. We are not blind to the worst but turn here to the finest examples of the native Ohio lands. There is an ulterior motive here for the best Ohio woods, wetlands and waters need protection. They need to be treasured. Taking you on this paper expedition through a book is hopefully the first stage of a longer journey. Press on, here in Ohio and in your homelands elsewhere. Humans are not the eternal enemy of Nature but only element in a landscape along with rocks and rainfall. Humans can do well by the landscape too. This comes home to us in Ohio so strongly because humans in the last two centuries have so altered our lands. But some people have also had the sense or the good fortune to hold some places untouched. Why this stewardship should have asserted itself at all is the greatest mystery of this book.

It becomes a question of families. When you look to the reserves or natural landmarks that survived, you come back to the families. And you come again to the great hardwood forest of Ohio history, the forest of Colonel Bouquet and the Indians he helped to pry loose. Patches of that ancient forest still stand in Ohio, perhaps 1,000 acres out of the original 25 million, but something remains. Nearly all of Ohio's ancient woods preserves are named for families—Gross, Hueston, Goll, Sigrist, Dysart. This was not merely out of vanity but because these natural wonders are truly manmade. Ohio's other natural wonders were always out-of-the-ordinary places—caves, islands, gorges, bluffs and fens. All of the ancient forest reserves were ordinary until over generations the non-action of *not* cutting the woods became a tangible act. Over time, doing nothing added up to the great deed of saving something.

We can never walk again in Ohio's ancient hardwood forest where a squirrel could supposedly jump branch to branch from the Ohio to Lake Erie but we can catch an inkling of it by studying the photographs of Ian Adams and by walking in the places that remain, places like the Dysart Woods Reserve in eastern Ohio's Belmont County. It's two woods really; twenty-six acres on one side of a ridge and then across the saddle, another twenty-six acres running down into a ravine. The trees are oak and sugar maple with a large number of beech and a few tulip poplars. The reserve which is managed by Ohio University is named for the Dysarts, but the family is all one stretching back to Miles Hart who emigrated here from Pennsylvania in 1813.

Neighbors to Miles Hart in those early were Thomas and Susannah Jackson who brought sheep with them into the forest. Thomas Jackson took up his axe to make Belmont County fit for sheep. Years later, Susannah remembered the nonstop burning of the great tree corpses. Thomas tended the log fires around the clock so to keep him company Susannah brought her spinning wheel out of their tiny cabin to work by firelight. The fires brought wolves to the edge of the forest. Susannah looked up from her distaff to see red eyes watching.

The wolves were long gone before the forest. Miles Hart had a daughter who married a Twinem, and their daughter married a Dysart. None of Henderson Dysart's four children ever married, but there were Dysart nieces to inherit. All these generations had one thing in common; they did nothing to the old woods draped on either side of the ridge.

The last Dysart was Gladys Dysart McGaughy who died in 1982. She would drive out to visit William Bartles, the volunteer caretaker who lived in the old Dysart farmhouse with his wife and children. Gladys Dysart McGaughy wasn't a yarn spinner or a compulsive talker, Bartles recalled. If you asked, she would tell you what she knew. But you had to ask. Bartles said that Gladys was a fund of information on the plants in the old woods but hard to pin down on the burning question that hovers over Dysart woods and all the other remnants—why was this piece held out?

The uncut land was steep, although steeper land was clear cut around it. The Dysarts were fairly prosperous. Glady's uncle, O.B. Dysart, was the last to farm the "home place," which covered 465 of Miles Hart's original 1,500 acres. "Now Gladys did tell me this," Bartles said. "Her uncle came to see her and asked, 'Well, should I have the last piece timbered?' Gladys knew what was in there but she also knew how to handle her uncle. 'Well, I don't know,' she said to him. 'Do you need the money?' Of course, that got him. 'Heaven sake, no!' 'Well then, just leave it alone.' Gladys told him."

That leaving alone left us with one of the finest stands of primeval oak forest on the continent. Dysart Woods was declared a National Natural Landmark in 1967. It draws to the backwoods of eastern Ohio visitors from all over the world including a pair of Oregon foresters who turned up on the Bartleses' doorstep in the teeth of a snowstorm. "I said, 'You're not going back there on a day like today,' " Bartles recalled. "But they said they'd come all this way to see virgin hardwood forest, and that's what they were going to do." The Oregonians disappeared into the storm and returned an hour later to the farmhouse to thaw out. The foresters were ecstatic, Bartles recalled. "They thought it was really something. These woods are as unique as their giant redwoods are out West. They said it was worth the trip."

The Ohio lands are worth the trip. It begins with these photographs by Ian Adams. Go slow. Look close.

Maples and beeches paint a tapestry of fall color on a hillside in Tinker's Creek Gorge in Bedford Reservation, one of the jewels in Cleveland's Emerald Necklace, a chain of 12 metroparks encompassing 19,000 acres which encircle the city.

1
A WALK IN THE WOODS

A FORTY-ACRE wood isn't big enough to be spooky, you decide on going in, even an ancient wood. True, these forty acres have never been cleared, never thinned and, except for mushrooms and the occasional windfall tree, never harvested. Which is why the Samuel G. Gross Natural Preserve exists at all, forty acres of primeval mixed hardwood surrounded by millions of acres of western Ohio cornfields. You wade in thinking that you can only get so lost in a forty acre wood.

Once inside, you rapidly lose all sense of direction in the thickets of ironwood. Gross Woods is a classic all-age stand; the natural order (or disorder) has not been "improved" so the old trees stand with saplings, the new-sprouted amidst the half-rotted. In full leaf, Gross Woods seems a temperate zone jungle. You can could only see so far. It's nothing like a California redwood grove where the giants stand like well-spaced cathedral pillars in a wide nave. Gross Woods is wetter, denser and a little unnerving.

Eventually you stumble out but you need your wits and your bearings in any Ohio woods, big or small. Primeval forest like Gross Woods may be rare and strictly circumscribed but Ohio is filling up again with woodland. Much marginal farmland has gone back to second and third growth forest; parks and natural preserves have expanded. Ohio is more densely wooded today than it has been in a century. When the native ecology is left alone, most of Ohio goes back to being what most of Ohio was before—-forest. These regrown woods harbor an amazing variety of trees, shrubs, wildflowers and mushrooms as well as forest critters—salamanders, woodpeckers, wild turkey and bugs.

A winter snowstorm eases its grip on hemlock trees and sandstone cliffs at Ritchey Ledges in the Cuyahoga Valley National Recreation Area in northeast Ohio. This 33,000-acre park along the lower stretches of the Cuyahoga River protects natural and historical areas providing a green "buffer-zone" between the industrial cities of Cleveland and Akron.

Today you can get lost in the Ohio woods (and you can certainly get hurt even in a small one), so honor the whiff of panic that comes over you in the deep shade. Make it a measure of respect. In parks, the trail runs on before you but often the a green wall of shrubs and tree trunks will shut you in on either side. Your footsteps become too loud. Flying things buzz round your head. Something sudden flicks through the leaf litter. A bird cries territorial limits but you can't make him out through the haze of branches. Stop. Be quiet. This is what you've come to see, to hear, to feel. Wide horizons are rare in the heartland forest but the press of native life is all around you. Be still in the woods.

Then come back in a month or in six. The Ohio woodscape appears and disappears as the calendar turns. Whole communities of wildflowers persist 51 weeks of the year for a week of flowering in May. The trees that induce green claustrophia in July lower their guard in December, revealing the sweep of once hidden terrain. A walk through an Ohio woods is like crossing the Greek philosopher's river; it is never the same twice.

Spring woods are theme and variation of every shade of green perceptible to the human eye: the feathery light green of new ferns, the red-streaked green of unrolling oak leaves and the hard green leather of may apples. Fall woods blaze up in their famous oranges and reds. In winter, the leaves make a fantastic Turkish carpet underfoot—pale brown, earth brown and rust brown. Winter woods are for those brave enough in mud and sure-footed on ice; summer woods for the gregarious and the sound of wind. In all seasons, bring some quiet with you.

Fall color highlights a woodland in Oak Openings Metropark near Toledo in northwest Ohio.
The Oak Openings, a series of sandy ridges interspersed with swampy areas, bogs, and wet prairies, are home
to more than 800 types of plants, including many rare and endangered species.

Asters and poison ivy herald the arrival of fall along roadsides in
northeastern Ohio. When the right conditions—warm, sunny days and cool
nights—occur during October, Ohio's fall color rivals the best
of New England's.

The Oak Openings area in northwestern Ohio is
a mushroom lover's delight, with hundreds of species
of fungi fruiting during wet periods in spring, summer,
and fall. This colorful mushroom is called the
viscid violet cortinarius.

Spring foliage clothes a sycamore tree along Clear Fork Gorge
in Mohican-Memorial State Forest in Richland County in
north-central Ohio. Clear Fork Gorge contains an extensive
beech-hemlock forest and is a designated National
Natural Landmark.

Brilliant scarlet leaves of smooth sumac add fall color to a hillside in Euclid Creek Reservation in the Cleveland Metroparks. This thickly wooded gorge was visited in 1915 by landscape architect Frederick Law Olmsted, Jr., who noted the "splendid quality of the scenery" and urged its preservation.

The venomous northern copperhead is widely distributed, though not common, in the hill country of southern Ohio. The tiny eastern massasauga rattlesnake and its larger cousin, the timber rattlesnake, are both endangered and have almost vanished from the Buckeye state.

A handsome male scarlet tanager takes a break during its northerly migration at Magee Marsh State Wildlife Area along Lake Erie in Ottawa County in northwestern Ohio. More than 300 species of birds have been recorded at Magee Marsh, which many regard as the finest birding area in the state.

Narcissus bloom in a woodland in the Cuyahoga Valley National Recreation Area in northeast Ohio. Nearby, a section of the recently-completed 22-mile Towpath Trail follows the course of the Ohio & Erie Canal through the valley.

Orange mycena mushrooms are among the most gaudy of the dozens
of species of fungi that can be found in summer and early fall in the woodlands and
meadows of Rocky River Reservation in the Cleveland Metroparks System.

Baby cottontail rabbits huddle together in a grassy field
at F. A. Seiberling Naturealm, a nature center and one of a dozen parks which
make up the Summit County Metroparks System in northeast Ohio.

Bird's-foot violet, named for the shape of the plant's leaves,
is one of many beautiful species of wildflowers which can be found
in April and May along forest roadsides in Shawnee State Park and Forest
in Scioto and Adams counties near Portsmouth in southern Ohio.

Kyle Woods State Nature Preserve, near Youngstown in Mahoning County,
is a fine example of the original Ohio hardwood forest which once covered this now densely-populated
and highly-industrialized area in northeastern Ohio.

A red-eyed vireo pauses during its search for insects at Magee Marsh State Wildlife Area in northwest Ohio. Part of the once vast Erie Marshes, this 1,821-acre preserve is an important staging area for migrating waterfowl and songbirds.

Red Maple trees glow in their autumn finery in Tinker's Creek Gorge, a National Natural Landmark in Bedford Reservation, part of the Cleveland Metroparks System which encircles the city in an "Emerald Necklace" for more than 80 miles.

Columbine flourishes on dolomite outcroppings in
Baker Fork Gorge at Fort Hill State Memorial, a 1200-acre preserve in Highland County.
In addition to the gorge and extensive woodlands, Fort Hill includes an earthworks
constructed by Hopewell Indians, who occupied the area from about
300 B.C. to 600 A.D.

The great-horned owl is the largest of Ohio's resident owl species. Others include the barred, screech, and, rarely, barn owls. During winter, long-eared, short-eared, and snowy owls are also frequent visitors to northern areas of the Buckeye state.

A red fox hunkers down in a woodland in Ashland County. The steady increase in eastern coyotes throughout the Buckeye state has not favored foxes, which must flee their territory or risk being killed by the larger coyotes.

Extirpated in Ohio by the early 1900s by overhunting and deforestation, the wild turkey or "gobbler" was reintroduced by the Ohio Department of Natural Resources during the 1950s and has made a spectacular comeback in heavily forested areas of eastern and southern Ohio.

A frigid winter day among the hemlocks and sandstone ledges at Ritchey Ledges in northeast Ohio. Hemlocks are found in cool ravines throughout the state, where they often grow to over 70 feet in height.

Redbud and dogwood, two sure signs of spring in the Buckeye state, flower along a forest road in Shawnee State Forest in Scioto County in southern Ohio. Shawnee is Ohio's largest contiguous forest, with more than 60 miles of hiking trails criss-crossing 60,000 acres of oak-hickory woodland.

A young raccoon poses reluctantly for the photographer after raiding a picnic area in Virginia Kendall Park, part of the 33,000-acre Cuyahoga Valley National Recreation Area in northeast Ohio. Raccoons are prolific inhabitants of parks and suburban backyards throughout the state.

The long-tailed
salamander is one
of the most handsome
of the 30-odd species
of salamanders which
can be found in the
Buckeye state.
This one was
photographed in a
woodland gorge in
Ashtabula County.

Red maple leaves create abstract patterns
below Blue Hen Falls, one of several scenic waterfalls
in the Cuyahoga Valley National Recreation Area in northeastern Ohio.
Downstream is another cascade, Buttermilk Falls.

2
IN WET PLACES

THE first time Ian Adams went to photograph the sphagnum peat bog at Triangle Lake, it was an experience out of "The African Queen." In the film, Humphrey Bogart was dragging a steamboat through an African swamp. In northeastern Ohio, Adams was dragging an old-fashioned view camera through the icy waters of a glacial kettle lake.

Triangle Lake is a classic sphagnum peat bog, a series of concentric circles whose outermost ring of open water is called the moat. It surrounds the edge of the peat "mat" and marks the point of no-return for plants that cannot live in the acid water created by the peat. The lake is in the eye of the ring.

By ecological logic, Triangle Lake is well out of its range, truly belonging to northern Michigan or southern Canada. But the town just down the road is Ravenna, Ohio, and Triangle Lake was here long before the town. This foreign landscape is a remnant of an older Ohio when the land hereabouts was fresh out of the retreating ice sheet. Until recent years when the state built a boardwalk access, the only way across the outer moat of Triangle Lake was to wade so when Adams and a photography buddy arrived, loaded up with tripods, bulky view cameras and waterproof bundles of film plates, they came prepared to walk out.

They had on fishing waders; the bog water went right over the tops. Lurching and cursing, the photographers floundered across the moat and up onto the quaking mat where the peat formed what passed for solid ground. They battled through a tangle of tamarack, blueberry and cranberry to reach the inner-most circle of the bog, the kettlehole lake itself. There Adams set up his view

A summer's day at Lake Katherine State Nature Preserve in Jackson County in southern Ohio. Lake Katherine, at 1,467 acres, is one of the largest of Ohio's more than 100 state nature preserves. It is home to Ohio's finest colony of big- leaf and cucumber magnolias, as well as the timber rattler.

camera. Suppressing shivers and all thoughts of the wade back, he opened his lens on this most foreign of natural Ohio landscapes.

Ian's pictures will take you dryshod to the heart of Ohio's wet places. It's an excellent vantage point to consider their variety—bogs, fens, prairies, kettle lakes, swamps, marshes and natural ponds of Ohio. Most are living memories of the last Ice Age, souvenirs of the departed continental glaciers. In northeastern Ohio, the glaciers left strings of pothole lakes, bogs and acid swamps. In northwest Ohio, the retreating glaciers created a series of ice-front lakes, all far larger than the present Lake Erie. When the "peri-glacial" lakes left behind a vast dead-flat, saturated drainage system the pioneers cursed as the Black Swamp. Along the Erie lakeshore were wide marshes filled with reeds and grasses, filled spring and summer with unnumbered migrating waterfowl. In the south, the Ohio twisted and turned through bottomlands of wide water meadows.

By any name—swamp or bog or marsh—wetlands were considered wastelands for nearly 200 years. Draining them was a matter of sound land management. Today Ohio has the dubious honor of being number two amongst the 50 states in the percentage of its original wetlands drained, paved or "improved" out of existence. Ohio has lost 95 percent of its original wetlands, putting it only a few points behind California in wetlands destruction. What remains is a fascinating tapestry of nearly vanished landscapes, of ecologies where water, earth and life are intricately mixed, and of "foreign" terrains that shouldn't be Ohio land but are. Get your feet wet.

Swamp rose mallow and swamp milkweed grow in abundance in the Lake Erie marshes around Sandusky Bay in northwestern Ohio. The beautiful pink or white flowers of the mallow are up to 8 inches across and form large colonies in mid-summer at marshy areas such as Magee Marsh State Wildlife Area.

Female mallard ducks take a nap on a pond that never freezes in Castalia near Sandusky Bay. Fed by artesian springs, this large pond provides open water and a haven for thousands of waterfowl during frigid northern Ohio winters.

Seen through a close-up lens, a fishing spider takes on epic proportions at Ottawa National Wildlife Refuge in northwest Ohio. Fishing spiders can hide underwater, and prey on insects, tadpoles, and even small fish.

A late winter snowstorm blankets a beaver pond in the Cuyahoga Valley National Recreation Area. This pond attracts nesting Canada geese and wood ducks, as well as mink, eastern coyotes, muskrats, and numerous herons, rails, and songbirds.

A beaver munches on a willow sapling in a pond in northeastern Ohio. Extirpated from Ohio by the 1830s by trapping, beaver reappeared in the 1930s and are now widely found in eastern Ohio, where they create valuable wetland habitat for many other species.

A male red-winged blackbird proclaims
its territory with a loud ock-a-lee from a willow
at Magee Marsh State Wildlife in Ottawa County in
northwestern Ohio. A sure sign of early spring in the
Buckeye State, red-winged blackbirds migrate
south in large flocks in the fall.

Tamarack trees turn gold in
late fall at Triangle Lake State
Nature Preserve in Portage
County in northeast Ohio.
This pristine 61-acre preserve
is one of the finest remaining
examples of a glacial kettle-
lake and boreal sphagnum
bog in the Buckeye state.
Significant plant species
include sundew, pitcher
plant, leather leaf, and
highbush blueberry.

33

A great blue heron stalks fish, frogs, and other prey at Ottawa National Wildlife Refuge in northwest Ohio. The Erie Marshes are a nesting area for at least 9 other species of herons, and large colonies of egrets and night herons nest on West Sister Island in Lake Erie.

Grass pink orchids bloom in June at Cranberry Bog State Nature Preserve, a 19-acre bog which floats, literally, in the waters of Buckeye Lake in Licking County in east-central Ohio. Formed from an ancient wetland which was flooded in the 1830's, the bog has abundant pitcher plants, sundews, and cranberries.

Killbuck Marsh Wildlife Area, which stretches across Wayne, Holmes, and Coshocton Counties in north-central Ohio, is Ohio's largest inland wetland. The 10,000-acre area is managed by the Ohio Division of Wildlife as key habitat for wood ducks, waterfowl, fur-bearing animals and many species of songbirds.

American lotus flowers in late summer at Seneca Lake in Noble County
in southeastern Ohio. Seneca Lake, with over 3,500 acres of water, is the largest of
the 10 eastern Ohio lakes managed by the Muskingum Watershed Conservancy
District for flood control, water conservation, and recreation.

Sunset at Ladue Reservoir in Geauga County in northeast Ohio.
Nearby are the headwaters of the Cuyahoga River as well as a thriving
community of Old-Order Amish, who farm in traditional fashion
using horse-drawn equipment and sweat.

A flock of tundra swans mixes with
Canada geese as the ice begins to melt in late
winter at Lake Pippin near Ravenna in Portage
County. Ohio is a major migration route for
these magnificent birds between their Arctic
breeding grounds and wintering areas
along the Atlantic coast.

A fiery dawn paints the
sky crimson at Frame Lake/
J. Arthur Herrick Fen State
Nature Preserve in Portage
County in northeast Ohio.
This 126-acre preserve
is a mosaic of wetlands,
including a lake, cattail
pond, tamarack
sphagnum bog, and
wet sedge meadow.

A dragonfly rests near a pond at
Tinker's Creek State Nature Preserve in Summit
and Portage Counties. In the background are the
bright purple flowers of ironweed, which puts
on a splendid show with goldenrod, Joe Pye weed,
asters, and other late summer wildflowers
in old fields throughout the
Buckeye state.

Sunrise looms through a
lingering fog at Stage's Pond
State Nature Preserve near
Circleville in Pickaway
County. This glacial kettle
lake is a favorite haunt of
migrating waterfowl and
songbirds.

Evening light in a wetland at Salt Fork State Wildlife Area, adjacent to Salt Fork State Park in Guernsey County in east-central Ohio. Salt Fork is the largest of Ohio's more than 70 state parks, and is a popular destination for many vacationing Ohioans throughout the year.

The sundew is a carnivorous plant
found in a few bogs in northern and central Ohio.
Insects are attracted to the sweet but sticky droplets
on the tentacles which radiate from the sundew's
club-shaped leaves. Once trapped, the insects are
digested by the sundew, which supplements
its diet within the nutrient-poor
bog environment.

Just a few miles from the urban metropolis of Columbus,
Gahanna Woods State Nature Preserve includes a swamp forest surrounded by
oak-hickory and beech-maple woodlands. Spring wildflowers include
yellow water crowfoot, swamp saxifrage, and several
species of trillium.

Showy lady's-slipper orchids bloom in
June at Gott Fen State Nature Preserve
in Portage County. This regal orchid,
very rare in Ohio, is one of 30-odd
orchid species native to
the Buckeye state.

A great egret surveys its territory at Ottawa National Wildlife Reserve near Lake Erie in northwest Ohio. Like its larger cousin, the great blue heron, the great egret finds plenty of fish, amphibians, and other prey in this 8,316-acre wetland refuge.

Fowler Woods State Nature Preserve in Richland County is host to one of Ohio's most spectacular displays of marsh marigolds, which cover several acres of wet woodland within the preserve during early spring. A mature beech-maple forest, with dozens of species of spring wildflowers, is another highlight of this 133-acre preserve.

The sun rises over the marshes of Ottawa National Wildlife Refuge
near Lake Erie in northwest Ohio. This remnant of the once-vast Lake Erie
marshes is an important stopover for migrating waterfowl and shorebirds.

3
GREAT LAKE EFFECTS

IT WAS shocking news in 1968, even if it was 15 years late and so garbled in the transmission that the world heard that Lake Erie was dead. It was the humble mayfly that died. On a stifling hot September day in 1953, the waters of western Lake Erie had stratified, sealing the billions of larval *Hexagenia limbata occulta*, the Lake Erie mayfly, in an oxygen-less bottom layer. The mayfly population crashed, and with it went the food base for the blue pike, cisco, white and lake trout, common species that had been harvested commercially by the millions of pounds. Without the mayfly, their populations crashed. And so it went, crash after crash, reverberating through the Lake Erie food chain, eventually wiping out Ohio's commerical fishermen who were the top feeders. This is when the media found out. The public was told that the lake had died. The confusion was understandable.

Lakes only die when they run out of water and with one-fifth of the planet's fresh water supply, the Great Lakes are in no danger of that. But Lake Erie, as the most southern and the most shallow of the Great Lakes, was vulnerable to environmental changes that were death to such species as the taken-for-granted mayfly and the once-prized blue pike. If news of the death of Lake Erie was exaggerated, the shock was healthy. It awoke Ohioans to the notion that Lake Erie was not limitless. It also reminded them how strongly the lake shapes the land.

TV weather reporters in northern Ohio call it the "lake effect." Most narrowly, it's a well documented meteorological mechanism; cold weather systems

Beach pea and dune grasses grow along an old fence at Headlands Dunes State Nature Preserve in Lake County. One of the few remaining beach and sand dune communities along Lake Erie's south shore, this small but significant natural area was dedicated in 1976 as an ecological research preserve.

moving southeast across Erie pick up lake moisture and release it inland against the rising Allegheny plateau. It throws places like the town of Chardon into localized snowbelts and affects the weather throughout the region in subtle ways. But there is a larger "lake effect" on northern Ohio. The lake affects nature systems along its margins. It affects the human presence too.

A central thesis here is that humans are part of Ohio's nature. Thus cities are also creations of nature. The lake, for example, made Cleveland, first as an outlet and then as a gathering place. In Cleveland and the great industrial cities around it, bulk commodities could be assembled to be merged such as iron and coal, or separated such as gasoline from crude oil. The railroads chose the lake's wide plain that ran westward with scarcely a hill between Cleveland and Chicago.

The "lake effects" then are multiple, ranging from the death of mayflies to the rise of great cities to the rising of maple sap in Chardon. Of all the original "natural" elements of Ohio—lake, rivers, forest, prairies—Lake Erie is in some ways the least changed. Its good moods and bad are its own affair; those who venture out on its waters must be humble and wary. Those who live inland keep an eye toward the water. But pollution and invasion have severely upset Lake Erie's balance. Along its shore, it takes a sharper eye to find the wild places—the sandy headlands, the grassy marshes and the valleys of once-clear rivers that still run northward in Ohio to the great lake and beyond to the wide Atlantic. But the lake is not dead.

The Lorain West Breakwater Light has guarded the entrance to
Lorain Harbor, west of Cleveland, for over 75 years. The light was built in
1917 by the U.S. Army Corps of Engineers. This winter view shows a large
flock of migrating mergansers in the open water near the lighthouse.

A large tree lies on the beach near Geneva, a victim of Lake Erie's destructive powers of shoreline erosion. The shallowest of the Great Lakes, Lake Erie is often whipped to a frenzy by summer thunderstorms and winter blizzards, which eat away at the fragile shale bluffs along the Ohio shore.

At first glance, these bright yellow plants look like common dandelions. In fact, they are Lakeside daisies, a globally rare species of wildflower found only in the old limestone quarries of the Marblehead peninsula in northwest Ohio. Nineteen acres of this rare habitat is now protected as Lakeside Daisy State Nature Preserve.

Kelleys Island includes many miles of pristine
Lake Erie shoreline, as well as the world's finest examples
of glacial grooves, gouged out of the island's limestone rock
by retreating glaciers during the Pleistocene era.

A great black-backed gull, as big as a small goose, struts along a Lake Erie beach in search of food. The great black-backed gull is an increasingly common winter visitor to Lake Erie, where it congregates with the smaller resident herring and ring-billed gulls.

Sunrise over the ice below the Marblehead Lighthouse in western Lake Erie. The shallower western basin of the lake is the first to freeze in winter, and the first to thaw in early spring.

The Marblehead lighthouse is the oldest lighthouse in Ohio,
as well as the oldest still in use on the Great Lakes. It was built in
1821, from native limestone, and stands 67 feet above the rocks.
A favorite haunt of artists and photographers, the lighthouse
is a pleasant place to while away a summer's hour.

Sunset over wetlands near Cedar Point in northwest Ohio.
Best known for its famous amusement park, the area also includes
several wetland preserves that are visited by large
numbers of waterfowl.

A pair of mute swans dance Swan Lake on the ice
near Sandusky. During late winter, open water near Sandusky Bay
is a favorite staging area for thousands of migrating ducks,
while thousands more gulls rest on the ice.

Pack ice forms ice castles along Lake Erie's shoreline at
Crane Creek State Park in northwestern Ohio. This park is a popular
destination for ice fishermen, who brave Lake Erie's frigid winter
weather to angle for walleye and yellow perch.

The Kelley Mansion on Kelleys Island was built
in the late 1800s by the island's founder for his son, Addison Kelley.
It boasts a suspended, spiral staircase and was a favorite
vacationing spot for several U.S. presidents.

An early morning view of downtown Cleveland from The Flats,
a restored area near the mouth of the Cuyahoga River and a major restaurant
and entertainment locale. In the foreground is the Anthony J. Celebrezze Fireboat,
which can pump up to 1500 gallons of water per minute from its hoses.

Sunrise over Sandusky Bay from the
south shore of Kelleys Island. Nearby,
though nearly erased by erosion, are
pictographs inscribed by Indians between
1200 A.D. and 1600 A.D. in a large block
of limestone called Inscription Rock.

4
RIVERLANDS

unning water carried America west by boat and by grist mill. At first, the inland rivers carried. Struggling overland across the Appalachians, the earliest emigrants prayed for the sight of the Ohio River where flatboats would provide a fast, one-way ticket into the interior. With the coming of steamboats, the Ohio became two-way—settlers in, products out. The Erie Canal bypassed the mountains and by the 1840s, travelers marveled at their rapid passage west by canal, lake steamer and the new trans-Ohio canals to the Ohio River. Rivertowns looked to great futures as they watched Cincinnati explode, the fifth largest city in the 1850s and the fastest growing, with steamboats and pork packinghouses.

The rivers were also engines; water power drove Ohio's first industrial revolution. Upstream, the water was set to work, feeding canals and powering mills. As the first sign of industrialization, the old mill stream was not always quaint; by mid-century, boomtowns like Akron and Springfield had rows of mills lining the raceways, piggy-backing on the water power and turning grain into flour, wood into furniture and iron into gadgets. But water power was not the future. Eventually railroads, Civil War and new industrial technology would drive Ohio in new directions.

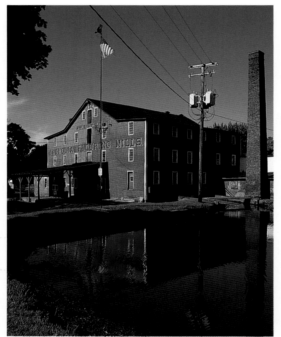

This 19th Century grist mill in Magnolia in Stark County is still operational, and is run by the fourth generation of the Elson family. Nearby is a section of the old Sandy & Beaver Canal, which linked the Ohio & Erie Canal with the Ohio River near East Liverpool.

In the late twentieth century, the ecological cost of Ohio's industrial revolution is clearer. The list of fish and molluscs that have been extirpated from Ohio waters reads "like one long dirge," according to the late Milton Trautman, the Fishman of Ohio, who waded and chronicled the decline of the state's waters in this century. Yet there are bright waters in Ohio still. Scenic river designations have protected the Little Beaver in eastern Ohio, the Little Miami in southwestern Ohio and the Big Darby in central Ohio. Elsewhere more people look to long-neglected rivers for recreation, for wildlife and for signs of balance. There is still no finer way to pass a summer's afternoon than following a backwoods Ohio creek upstream, watching for crayfish and kingfishers or skimming flat stones across the pools.

Ohio's first water technology of canals and mills has acquired a graceful patina of age. The state has seven functioning water-powered grist mills including Clifton Mill, the largest working mill in this country. Small sections of restored canal near Coschocton and Piqua are working again, hauling schoolkids and tourists around historic parks. The canals and the mills reminds us that the running waters made Ohio. Protecting them will make Ohio anew.

Brandywine Falls is the largest of many waterfalls
in the Cuyahoga Valley National Recreation Area. Several mills
operated near the falls during the 1800s, including a grist mill, a sawmill,
a woolen mill, and a distillery which turned out 30 to 40 gallons
a day of "excellent whiskey."

This Clifton Gorge photograph, taken in the same
vicinity as the opposite winter scene three months later,
illustrates the dramatic seasonal changes that
occur in the Ohio lands.

The Little Miami River cascades through
Clifton Gorge State Nature Preserve in
Greene County in southwestern Ohio.
Abundant wildflowers, the tumbling
river, and tall cliffs of dolomite make this
one of the most scenic and botanically
diverse areas in the Buckeye state.

Fisherman test their skill on the Ohio
River at Marietta, established in 1788 as
Ohio's earliest settlement and city, and the gateway
to the Northwest Territory. The city was named for
Queen Marie Antoinette, as thanks to France
for its support during the
Revolutionary War.

A bird's-eye view of Ripley, a historic town
on the Ohio River, from the Rankin House, where more
than 2,000 slaves, fleeing from southern plantations, found sanctuary
at this Underground Railroad home of Reverend John Rankin
and his wife, Jean, from 1828 until 1863.

Scarlet leaves of smooth sumac frame a view
of the Ohio River at Gallipolis, the county seat of Gallia County
in southern Ohio. Nearby, at Rio Grande, is the 1,100-acre Bob Evans
Farm, home from 1953 to 1971 to Bob Evans, the sausage
maker and restauranteur.

Snow-covered hemlocks bend toward Mill Creek in the western suburbs of Youngstown in Mahoning County. The Mill Creek Park Metropolitan Park District includes 2,530 acres of scenic woodlands, lakes, streams, and gardens in this hilly industrial city in northeastern Ohio.

Originally built in 1861, Indian Mill was the nation's first museum of milling. It is located on the Sandusky River near Upper Sandusky in rural Wyandot County. An earlier mill was built nearby in 1820 for the Wyandot Indians in gratitude for their support during the War of 1812.

This scenic 30-foot waterfall is located
on the grounds of the West Milton Inn, a popular destination
for diners in the village of West Milton in Miami
County in southwestern Ohio.

Lanterman's Mill,
located in Youngstown's Mill Creek
Park, has been restored to a working grist
mill, and visitors can buy corn and wheat
ground with power from a 14-foot oak
water wheel located inside the mill.
Nearby is a scenic waterfall and
a covered bridge.

The Shawnee Princess is one
of the few steam-powered
riverboats remaining in the
Buckeye State. It is moored
at Providence Metropark on
northwest Ohio's Maumee
River, and provides visitors
during the summer with an
hour-long trip up and
down the Maumee.

Clifton Mill, built in 1802 and one of the largest grist mills ever
built in the U.S., is located in the picturesque village of Clifton in Greene County
near Springfield. The mill is operational and includes a fine restaurant,
picnic area, and gift shop, where you can buy pancake mixes,
stone-ground wheat flour, and cornmeal.

This delightful century-old suspension bridge
was built in 1895 over Mill Creek in what is now
Mill Creek Park in Youngstown, Ohio.

Pebbles, tumbled around
like clothes in a drier by the
cascading waters of Greenville
Creek, created these potholes
in the limestone rock at
Greenville Falls State Nature
Preserve in Miami County
near Covington.

Below 100-foot shale bluffs, Tinker's Creek rushes through
the depths of Tinker's Creek Gorge in Cleveland's Bedford Reservation
en route to its confluence downstream with the Cuyahoga River.

A bird's-eye view of Marietta,
Ohio's first settlement, at the confluence of
the Ohio and Muskingum rivers in Washington County.
In the town's Mound Cemetery is an Indian mound,
as well as the graves of more Revolutionary War
officers than any other place in America.

The Muskingum River,
photographed here in
late summer near Dresden
in Muskingum County,
is the largest river
wholly contained within
the Buckeye State. Formed
by the junction of the
Walhonding and Tuscarawas
Rivers, it joins the Ohio
River at Marietta in
Washington County.

An evening view of Cincinnati, dubbed by
Longfellow the "Queen City of the West," from
across the Ohio River in Devou Park, Kentucky.
Winston Churchill described Cincinnati as
"America's most beautiful inland city."

5
THE GREAT PLAIN

Mention the Ice Age to Ohio school children and many an eye glazes over. In school, the glaciers roll over childish minds so often that the smartest soon learn that the best answer (or at least the best guess) to any Ohio geography question is, "The glaciers." Jane Forsyte who taught geology for 30 years at Bowling Green State University saw the glacial effect on her otherwise well-informed neighbors. "They thought everything in Ohio was caused by glaciers," she recalls, "even the coal."

The glaciers had nothing to do with Ohio coal (or at least nothing obvious). But they were largely responsible for one of Ohio's most spectacularly unspectacular characteristics—its flatness. Interstate 71 which runs from Cincinnati through Columbus to Cleveland sketches out the rough imprint of the Wisconsian glacier on Ohio. It left the northern and western two-thirds of the state under a deep blanket of glacial till, soil picked up by the ice and dropped as it melted back. The flat, flat till soil plain yields Ohio's other visual cliche—corn as high as the Fourth of July. Glaciers leave great, great soil behind.

The rich plains have delighted Ohio farmers ever since they peeled the primeval forest cover back and plowed into glacier-delivered minerals layered under 10,000 years of leaf mulch. Rich farmland may be poor sight-seeing for non-farming tourists but the observant can watch Ohio's great central plain unwind in long, graceful swells. Especially in western Ohio, the sky has room to unroll from horizon to horizon.

Columbus is the great city of Ohio's great plain. It was founded in a real estate deal as the capital city because its central location and flat approaches made it accessible. But Columbus also drew on the great riches of the flat plains around it. The Ohio State University was founded as much for an agricultural college as for teaching the less immediately useful arts and sciences. "Millions for manure," quipped one of James Thurber's OSU English professors at the turn of the century, "but not one cent for Art." The taunt is not only outdated but ironic. In the last century, Columbus grew on the manure of agriculture and state politics while the rest of Ohio ran blast furnaces and made shoes. In recent decades, Ohio's heavy manufacturing has run into trouble and her metal-working cities have felt the loss. Meantime, Columbus devoted itself to the electronic arts, processing information not iron ore. Those arts have turned to millions.

Ohio Spiderwort blooms in
early summer along a roadside near Marion
in north-central Ohio.

A solitary tree stands in a soybean field in Fulton
County in what was once the fearsome Great Black Swamp
which covered much of northwestern Ohio. The swamp was drained
in the late 1800s, leaving only the giant burr and chinquapin oaks
of nearby 40-acre Goll Woods State Nature Preserve as a
reminder of Fulton County's original natural terrain.

The century-old church of Mount Tabor, near
West Liberty in rural Logan County, was built as a
Methodist Church in 1881, and is now used as a meeting
place where local residents narrate the history of this
scenic area to visitors and school groups. The famed
frontiersman, Simon Kenton, spent his last years
in nearby Zanesfield.

Twenty acres of giant sunflowers keep an eye
on the sun in Perry County in east-central Ohio.
Widely cultivated for their rich seeds and oil, sunflowers
are a common sight in summer in the Buckeye State.

Early morning in a field of wheat stubble in midsummer
near Wauseon in Fulton County in northwest Ohio. Corn, wheat, and
soybeans are the principal crops in Ohio's western plain.

Flowers frame a view of Castle Piatt Mac-O-Chee,
built after the Civil War by Colonel Donn Piatt near
West Liberty in Logan County. Another castle, Castle Piatt
Mac-O-Cheek, built by Donn's brother General Abram
Piatt, rises out of the woods a mile to the west.
Both are open to the public.

Twenty-three ancient Indian burial mounds are preserved at Mound City National Monument near Chillicothe in Ross County. The mounds were built by the Moundbuilders, Hopewell and Adena Indians who laid claim to the surrounding real estate from about 300 B.C. to 600 A.D.

A giant burr oak lies in a woodland pool at Drew Woods State Nature Preserve in Darke County, a tiny remnant of the vast oak forests that once covered much of Ohio.

A Mail Pouch barn, near a wheatfield in rural Williams County,
evokes an era when chewing tobacco had not lost its social respectability.
Ohio has more Mail Pouch barns than any other state.

One of several resident cats reclines
on the steps of the farmhouse at Slate Run
Living Historical Farm in Pickaway County south
of Columbus. The site is an active recreation
of farm life in central Ohio in
the 1880s.

A view of downtown
Columbus from the west
bank of the Olentangy
River. Ohio's State
Capital and largest city,
Columbus is a major
center of commerce,
government, and trade.

Bigelow Cemetery State Nature Preserve, like its neighbor Smith Cemetery, preserves a small piece of Ohio's pioneer history and native tallgrass prairie plants in the midst of farms and cornfields in central Ohio's rural Madison County.

Purple coneflowers and wild bergamot fill the tiny,
1/2-acre Smith Cemetery in the Darby Plains west of Columbus.
This pioneer cemetery and remnant of Ohio's tallgrass prairie
was dedicated in 1982 as a State Nature Preserve.

A late fall day along Big Darby
Creek west of Columbus. The
Darby Creek system, a major project
of the Ohio Chapter of The Nature
Conservancy, is one of the most
pristine riverine systems in the
United States.

May apples grow beneath a grove of old-growth tulip trees
at Davey Woods State Nature Preserve in Champaign County.
The preserve was established in 1990 with help from
the Davey Tree Expert Company and the Ohio
Chapter of The Nature Conservancy.

Wild Lupine and Yellow Puccoon
bloom at the Kitty Todd Preserve in
Lucas County in Ohio's "Oak Openings."
Managed by The Nature Conservancy's
Ohio Chapter, the area is home to rare
plants and insects, including the Karner
blue butterfly.

A glacial lake, a remnant of the last ice age,
fills a hollow in the rolling farm country near
West Liberty in Logan County.

6
HILLS AND HOLLOWS

The New Yorker writer John McPhee has described the topography of Ohio as looking like a rumpled bedspread on which someone has had a quick nap. The napper was the Ice Age and the southeastern third of Ohio missed the blanket of ice-born soil and debris. Sometimes called "Ohio's Outback," the southeast is our most rugged landscape, a terrain of sharp valleys, steep hills, thin soils and rushing waterfalls.

The bare bones of Ohio geology are visible in the Outback. That geology has been bountiful and cruel. The southeast was the first part of the territory open to settlement and land-hungry farmers from Virginia and Kentucky swarmed north of the Ohio. The thin soils could not withstand intensive agriculture. Farms in the southeast were eroding away and being abandoned long before the turn-of-the-century, leaving behind hard scrabble land, regrowth forest and coal. That is the region's second gift or curse. To get at the coal, the choice is human suffering in deep mining or ecological suffering in strip mining. Neither lies easy on the land. Driving the southeast today, you can to wind through a valley of lush woods, crest a small hill and drop into a moonscape of strip pits. Some of the worst mining abuses have been curbed but the sores are all the more painful against the resurgent native woods.

Geology also gave southeastern Ohio its hollows and waterfalls. Water has had the "deep time" of tens of thousands of years to slice out valleys, uncover ledges and leave precarious overhangs. The rugged terrain and its depopulation have made the southeast the wildest quarter of Ohio. Today it is the most heavily wooded, checkerboarded with state parks, the Wayne National Forest and vast private holdings. The southeast was the first to see the return of the beaver and the wild turkey, which were all but extirpated from Ohio by the turn-of-the-century. Even the

A misty morning at Blue Rock State Park in Muskingum County near Zanesville. Deep in the woods of the surrounding Blue Rock State Forest, this remote park offers solitude and room for hiking, nature study, or just plain relaxation.

occasional black bear has been spotted in recent years on forays across the Ohio River from the West Virginia. The wildness makes the southeast the land of last hope for many of Ohio's endangered fish, mussels, insects and amphibians. Scientists comb the hills and riverbeds, looking for hold-out populations.

Being the first territory settled, the southeast is home to Ohio's first city, Marietta, and to its oldest college town, Athens. Marietta is an amazing place, a blend of American history and Yankee anthropology. The men behind the Ohio Company which secured the first land grant, were New Englanders and former officers in Washington's Army. As men of some learning, they brought New England ways and Latin tags to the frontier. They called their first fort, the Campus Martius, but being frugal Yankees, built the first homes close together as blockhouses, joined by wooden walls. When the Indian threat receded, they took down the walls and had the street grid ready to hand. Then came the flood of mountain folk out of Kentucky and Virginia, hard-handed buckskinners with little respect for Yankee religion or gentry. That cultural conflict roiled the southeast for a century but Marietta still has something of the whiggish airs of its Revolutionary War founders about it.

Athens is the Berkeley of the Midwest (or is it the other way around?), founded on classical learning and continued on the belief that the rest of the world is slightly out-of-touch. This is part of the Athens attraction. Athens is really two towns, the student Athens which exists from fall to spring when it disperses to the winds. Then Appalachian Athens emerges from the shadows, a courthouse town and regional commercial hub that was there all along, dealing in lawsuits, farm machinery, wood products and a lot of handicrafts. Come fall, it is buried again in students.

An ice storm creates beauty and slippery footing
along the trail to Cedar Falls in the Hocking Hills. Downstream,
along Queer Creek, are some of Ohio's largest hemlock trees.

Pines cling to the sandstone rimrock of Conkles Hollow
State Nature Preserve in Ohio's scenic Hocking Hills.
Named for W. J. Conkle, who carved his name into the west wall
in 1794 or 1797, this 87-acre area was dedicated as a state
nature preserve in 1977.

Floral symbols of spring in Ohio's rugged
hill country, dogwood and redbud bloom together
in a woodland at Lake Hope State Park in Vinton
County. Nearby are the remains of Hope Furnace,
one of dozens of iron ore blast furnaces which
operated in this area during the 1800s. The iron
industry in this area faded out after the Civil War.

A hemlock spreads its roots like an octopus around a
boulder of Black Hand sandstone in Queer Creek in Hocking
County. Located between Old Man's Cave and Cedar Falls, this rugged
gorge is a hiker's delight, with many waterfalls, huge hemlocks,
and spectacular rock formations.

Morning mist rises from the remote ridges
of Shawnee State Forest in Scioto County. Sprawling
across 60,000 acres, Shawnee is the largest unbroken
expanse of woodland in Ohio. Often called the
"Little Smokies," it includes more than 50 miles
of hiking trails and 60 miles of bridle trails,
as well as an 8,000-acre wilderness area.

Cedar Falls is one of several waterfalls
in the Hocking Hills, arguably the most
scenic area in the Buckeye State. The falls
were named for the tall hemlocks, the
pioneers didn't know their trees, which
are abundant in the gorge below the falls.

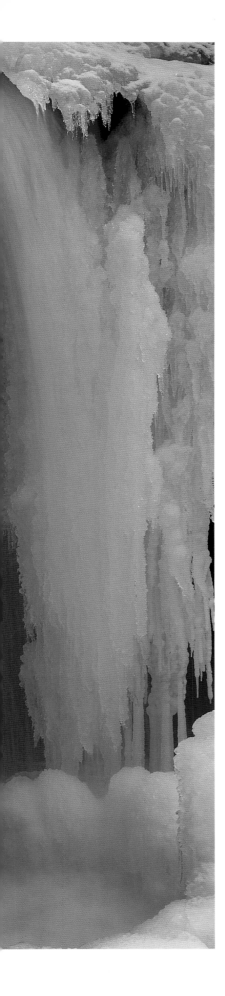

Ash Cave isn't really a cave at all, but Ohio's
largest recessed sandstone overhang, towering more than 90 feet
and spanning more than 300 feet. It was named for the ashes
left by ancient Indians, and has an intermittent
waterfall, which in severe winters can form
an impressive ice cone.

Hosak's Cave, like its larger neighbor, Ash Cave in the Hocking
Hills, is a recessed sandstone cave in Salt Fork State Park in
Guernsey County in east-central Ohio. Salt Fork, Ohio's largest state
park, has facilities for hiking, boating and fishing as well
as a campground and lodge.

Emerging spring foliage paints the canvas of a hillside at
Conkles Hollow State Nature Preserve. The Rim Trail along the top
of the massive 200-foot sandstone cliffs which edge the gorge
is one of Ohio's most thrilling hikes and includes some
of the finest views in the state.

The Crested Dwarf Iris is common in Ohio's
southeastern hill country during spring. In late spring and early
summer its larger cousin, the Blue Flag, blooms in
wetland areas throughout the state.

This magnificent spring view of hills and hollows is from Jacob's Ladder,
a sandstone outcrop at Christmas Rocks State Nature Preserve in Fairfield County.
The county also has one of the largest concentrations of covered bridges
remaining in the Buckeye State.

These old coke ovens, now surrounded by woods and wildflowers,
once fed the flames of the Vinton Iron Furnace near McArthur in Vinton County.
More than 40 of these blast furnaces once operated in the area, known as
the Hanging Rock Iron Region.

Cedar Falls cascades over limestone rocks near the tiny village of
Cedar Mills in southern Ohio's Adams County. The rugged gorge through which
Cedar Run wends its way has an abundance of arbor vitae, or northern white
cedar, and is owned by the Ohio Chapter of The Nature Conservancy.

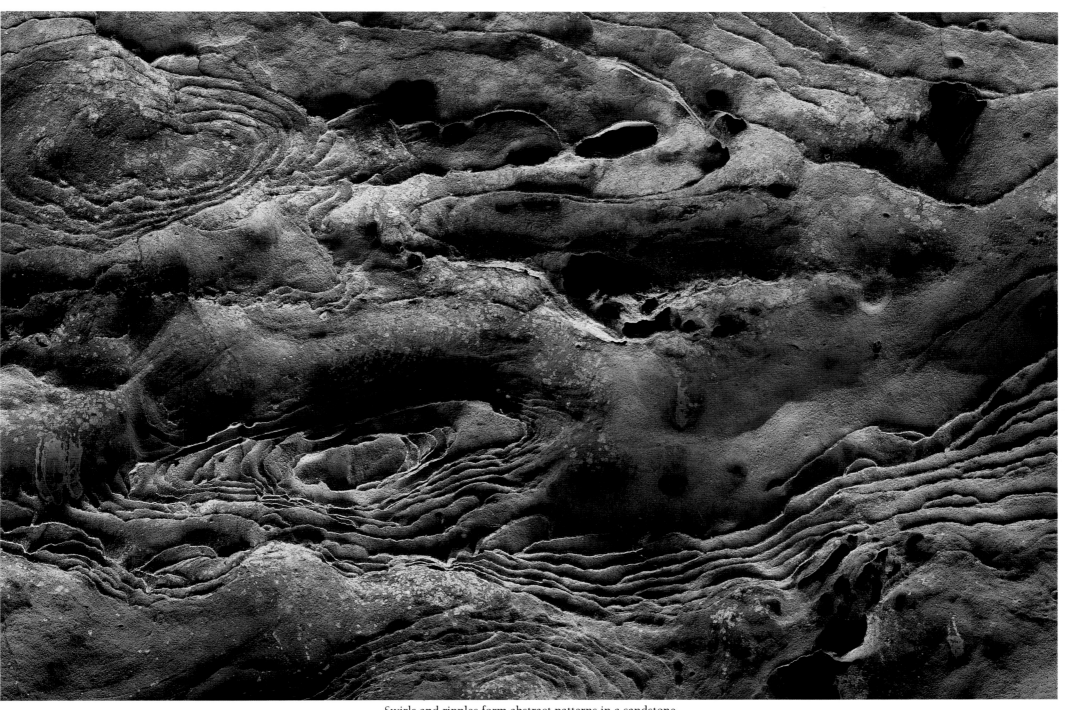

Swirls and ripples form abstract patterns in a sandstone
overhang near Big Pine Road in Hocking County. The rock was
formed from coarse sand and sediment deposited more
than 300 million years ago.

7
GOING TO THE COUNTRY

I T IS the ancestral farm of the American mind—a white farmhouse, a red barn, fields of corn, cows for milk, pigs for market, chickens for egg money and a pond for relief. It occupies a heritage landscape which was the slow work of generations of farmers and their domestic animals. Cutting, grazing and planting, they smoothed the land into this familiar shape. It is our contention that a heritage landscape like this is "natural" in Ohio. Yes, it is man-made but so was "wild" prairie, burnt by tribal peoples who "farmed" the prairie animals with fire. It is a European landscape, formed by centuries of practice, but modified in the New World to new conditions. In Ohio towards the turn-of-the-century, it reached a classical form; 100 or so acres, a few machines, a few cows, many pigs or chickens, a team of horses and one family.

Whether this traditional farm scene is from your memory or your great-grandfather's is almost irrelevant. It derives from a time when most Americans farmed or still had relatives who did. Whether it dates from a hard childhood of gathering eggs and chopping weeds, a summer visiting country cousins or whether it is fourth-hand through a book, the look and rhythms of this heritage farm are soaked deep in our national memory. The purest form of this rural dreamscape was the midwestern family farm. And the purest form of that was and still is to be found in Ohio.

A country road snakes its way past farms and wooded ridges in early fall in Washington County near Marietta. Nearby is the Wayne National Forest, the only national forest in the Buckeye State, covering 178,000 acres of Appalachian foothills in 10 southeastern Ohio counties.

Changes in technology and economics are reshaping that rural landscape but the archetype is still visible in Ohio, especially in the Amish regions of central Ohio. The Amish people are not the subject here. We are referring to the Amish farmlands and not to the people. Their quaint clothing is only a sign of their Anabaptist religious beliefs that have held them out of our technological torrent. But their horse-drawn buggies are a sign of their apartness from "English" (i.e. other Americans, from British to Chinese) ways. The horse is part of the reason Amish culture has preserved this heritage rural landscape. The Amish still measure their ambitions and their holdings by what one family with limited machinery and good draft horses can manage. Strangely enough, the Amish avoidance of debt, chemicals, expensive machines and non-family help has left their farms among the strongest economically in Ohio. On Ohio's Amish and non-Amish backroads, you can see farming as a preservative of landscape.

The other two great treasures of the old rural scene are the barn and the covered bridge. Ohio has a wealth of both. Neither is considered economically vital today. Modern farm buildings house expensive machines or machine-like animals being raised under factory conditions. The old barns stuffed with hay and alive with cats are too big to paint and to replace these days. The covered bridge is even more obsolete. That's all the more reason to see them here.

A goat regards the
photographer with a
quizzical stare in a barn
at Sauder Farm and
Craft Village near Archbold
in Fulton County. Local
businessman and historian
Erie Sauder founded this
living farm museum
and restored pioneer village
which features glassblowing,
woodcarving, spinning,
weaving, and dozens of
other pioneer crafts.

Sunrise along a country road
in rural Vinton County near Mount
Pleasant, a far cry from the urban bustle
of Columbus, a scant 60 miles away.
Nearby is Zaleski State Forest, which offers
miles of hiking and bridle trails in
this remote section of the
Buckeye State.

95

An evening view of
Lancaster in Fairfield
County from the craggy
heights of Mount
Pleasant. Within the
city's historic district is
the Sherman House,
the birthplace of Civil
War General William
Tecumseh Sherman.

A summer sunrise
burns through the
morning mist over farm
fields near Bellefontaine in
Logan County. Legendary
frontiersman and Indian
fighter Simon Kenton once
lived in this area, near
the headwaters of the
Mad River.

This beautiful octagonal house, based on a design by Thomas Jefferson, stands near the village of Windsor in rural Ashtabula County in northeast Ohio. Built in 1846, the house is currently occupied by an Amish family and is one of five octagonal houses remaining in the county.

Malabar Farm in Richland County, now a state park, is perhaps best known as the place where movie stars Humphrey Bogart and Lauren Bacall married and honeymooned in May 1945.

Visitors often exclaim "Jeez," when they admire the view of Malabar Farm from this lofty hilltop, appropriately named "Mount Jeez." Malabar, which means "beautiful valley" in an Indian dialect, is where author and farmer Louis Bromfield developed his innovative method of "grass farming," a system of sowing grasses in certain areas to prevent erosion and enrich the ground.

Chickens watch the world go by from their perch on the window sill of an Amish barn near Charm in the rolling hills of Holmes County, center of the world's largest population of Amish and a major tourist attraction during summer months.

Sturdy work horses graze on a hill in early spring at an Amish farm near Fredericksburg in Wayne County. Horse-power and hard manual labor is the basis of the traditional Amish farming methods used to grow corn, wheat, and oats.

Ohio has about 125 covered bridges remaining, second only to Pennsylvania. One of the most scenic is this elegant Humpback Bridge, built over Raccoon Creek in an isolated corner of rural Vinton County. This 165-foot, three-span structure was built in 1874 to replace an earlier bridge.

The Geauga County Historical Society established this Century Village on 60 acres of farmland south of the village green in Burton. The village includes century homes, two churches, an 1872 one-room schoolhouse, a Victorian dress-maker's shop, a railroad station, and a farm complex.

This charming windmill was built by Jim Beam
and moved from a farm in Mount Vernon, Ohio to
its present location at Bob Evans Farm near Rio Grande
in Gallia County. Once used to grind corn
and other grains, the windmill is now
powered by an electric motor.

One of Ohio's most scenic
covered bridges is the Warner
Hollow Bridge, built in 1867
over Phelps Creek near Windsor
in Ashtabula County. Thirteen
other bridges still stand in the
county, evoking the nostalgia
of a bygone era.

The fine old Hills Bridge spans the Little Muskingum River in
Washington County near Marietta. Built in 1878 and closed to traffic in 1990,
the bridge features a Howe truss. Nearby are several other scenic
covered bridges in Washington and Monroe Counties.

The magnificent Manchester round barn is one of the
largest and most beautiful ever built in the U.S. The barn, built by
Jason Manchester in 1908, is located east of New Hampshire in Auglaize County.
It measures 102 feet in diameter, has three levels, and is now used by the
fourth generation of Manchesters.

An Amish farm and pond glow in late afternoon
winter sunlight near Charm in Holmes County. Note
the two houses, typical of Amish farms. Retired
grandparents live in one of them and participate
in the daily life of the farm as they are able, cherished
and cared for by the younger members of the family—the
Amish have no need for retirement homes
and Social Security!

An octagonal barn, one of perhaps 30 round and
polygonal barns remaining in the Buckeye State,
stands on a farm in Miami County in western Ohio.
Most of Ohio's round barns were built during the
late 1900s and early 20th-century. As many as 120
of these distinctive barns survive in neighboring
Indiana, which leads the nation in round and
polygonal barns.

Sheep stare down the photographer
on the Moore farm near Piedmont in east-central Ohio's
Harrison County. This county was heavily strip-mined for
coal earlier this century, but much of the land has reverted
to timber and family farms. Several generations of
the Moore family raise sheep in this quiet
corner of the Buckeye State.

This Amish farm is near Jelloway in Knox County,
on the fringes of Ohio's Amish community, the largest
in the world. The sheaves of wheat or oat stalks are stacked
in the fields during summer, dried, and later used as
livestock bedding.

The Louis Bromfield House and garden at Malabar Farm.
Known as the "Big House," the 32-room house includes nine bedrooms,
six full bathrooms, and four half-bathrooms. The original
furnishings are still in place, and many of the rooms have special
door latches Bromfield installed to allow his beloved
boxer dogs to roam the house.

Horses frolic in the pastures of a farm in New Bedford, an
Amish community in Coshocton County. While many bemoan the
plight of the American farmer, the Amish virtues of hard work,
frugality, interdependence, and common "horse" sense enable them
to prosper while their "English" counterparts struggle to
maintain the family farm.

This old barn stands alongside a busy highway
near the village of Bournville in Ross County. Rural Ohio offers a treasure
trove of English, Dutch, round, polygonal, log, and Pennsylvania
bank barns for the barn enthusiast.

8
GOING TO TOWN

IT'S called Plymouth Street which was always a grander name than the road itself which was always dirt when it was not mud. It is still dirt, still running uphill to a stagecoach inn built around 1830 in the village of Hanoverton in Columbiana County. Visually it is still 1830 on Plymouth Street. Through luck, the grace of being forgotten, and a careful modern restoration, Plymouth Street preserves an early Ohio townscape—the travelers' town. The state is dotted with them—canal towns, river towns, railroad towns and early motoring towns. Few are as easy to recognize as Plymouth Street but the modern traveler can learn to spot faint clues—the Race Streets in so many old milling towns, the boarded-up tourist cabins and filling stations growing weeds in by-passed highway towns or the extra-wide Main Streets laid out so that a teamster could turn his horse-drawn freight wagon in one move.

Many Ohio towns and small cities still have their origins written as plainly on their faces as freckles on an Irishman. There are the farm towns like Chardon, for example, where farmers of the Geauga County have been coming for two centuries to buy, sell, borrow, vote, ship, receive goods and seek justice. Once their kids came to town for higher schooling; their wives for printed

Cincinnati's "Over-The-Rhine" district includes the largest collection of 1900s Italianate architecture of any city in the U.S. With help from organizations such as the Cincinnati Preservation Association, many of these fine buildings have been rescued and restored.

textiles and something to read. Now visitors come each fall supposedly to watch the farmers boil maple tree sap in syrup but, in truth, to remember the land. The Ohio county was a horse-sized unit; the county seat could be no farther than a day by buggy from any corner. Today's towns are awkwardly sized for cars but the courthouse, even in entirely urban counties like Cuyahoga, still marks the older limit.

These units and the early forms of Ohio towns derived from natural measures—a horse's pace, the path of a river, the failure of a harvest in Ireland. Other grew on their exploitation of distant landscapes; Springfield became the reaper-building capital for the far-off harvesters of the Great Plains. Many of those first industries are long gone but their marks are on the townscape, if you can see them.

Many elements drive a town, even dreams, and Ohio in the last century was overrun by town-building dreamers. They built Zoar as a communal enterprise or they settled Kirtland as a Mormon refuge from eastern persecution. Religion or education (or sometimes both) were behind the ordering of a dozen college towns. Now the old red brick halls of academe sit upon the Ohio landscape as if they were there forever.

Sandusky, gateway to Lake Erie,
was first settled by Connecticut Yankees, whose
homes were burned by British coastal raiders during the
Revolutionary War, giving the surrounding area its name,
the Firelands. Nearby is Cedar Point, one of the
nation's premier amusement parks.

Architecture buffs come from all over
to see this 1917 masterpiece, the Peoples Federal
Savings and Loan Building in Sidney in western Ohio.
This elegant structure, with its terra cotta inlays
and gilded lions, was designed by Louis Sullivan,
known as the "father of the modern
skyscraper."

Historic Quaker Square in downtown Akron
is where German immigrant Ferdinand Schumacher
began his grain empire in the 1800s, the forerunner of the
Quaker Oats Company. Today, the century-old grain silos
are guest rooms in the Quaker Square Hilton hotel,
and the grain factory buildings house a
shopping mall and restaurant.

A 1973 Ford truck adds a period touch
to a scene along Main Street at Shawnee,
an old mining town in Perry County.

The Historic District of Mt. Pleasant,
located near the Ohio River in
Jefferson County, was placed on the
National Register of Historic Places
in 1974. The town was a center
for anti-slavery acrtivities and
had many "stations" on the
underground railroad.

The Harding Memorial in Marion
is a circular monument of Georgia marble
containing the stone coffins of U.S. President
Warren G. Harding and his wife, Florence Kling Harding.
This stately building, which cost $700,000, is
surrounded by ten acres of landscaped
grounds.

An astounding 113 of the buildings
in the Lorain County town of Wellington
are on the National Register of Historic Places, including
the "Spirit of '76" Museum, commemorating
Archibald Willard's painting, one of the best known
patriotic paintings ever produced in
the United States.

Ohio is often called the "mother of presidents"—seven of the ten U.S. Presidents
who served in the white house between Reconstruction and the Roaring Twenties
were born in the Buckeye State. The McKinley Library in Niles
is a tribute to the 25th U.S. President, William McKinley,
who was born here on January 29, 1843.

Wittenberg University,
established in 1845 at Springfield
in Clark County, is one of 48 independent,
non- profit liberal arts colleges in Ohio.
There are also 13 state universities
and many other community and technical
colleges and schools throughout
the Buckeye State.

Plymouth Street at Hanoverton is virtually unchanged
from the 1830s, when this was a booming canal town in Columbiana
County along the Sandy and Beaver Canal, which linked the
Ohio & Erie Canal with the Ohio River.

The Italian villa-inspired Dayton Art Institute in Montgomery County
features contemporary art, a noteworthy collection of European paintings, and a
fine East Asian wing. In nearby Dayton, Orville and Wilbur Wright
nurtured their dreams of manned flight.

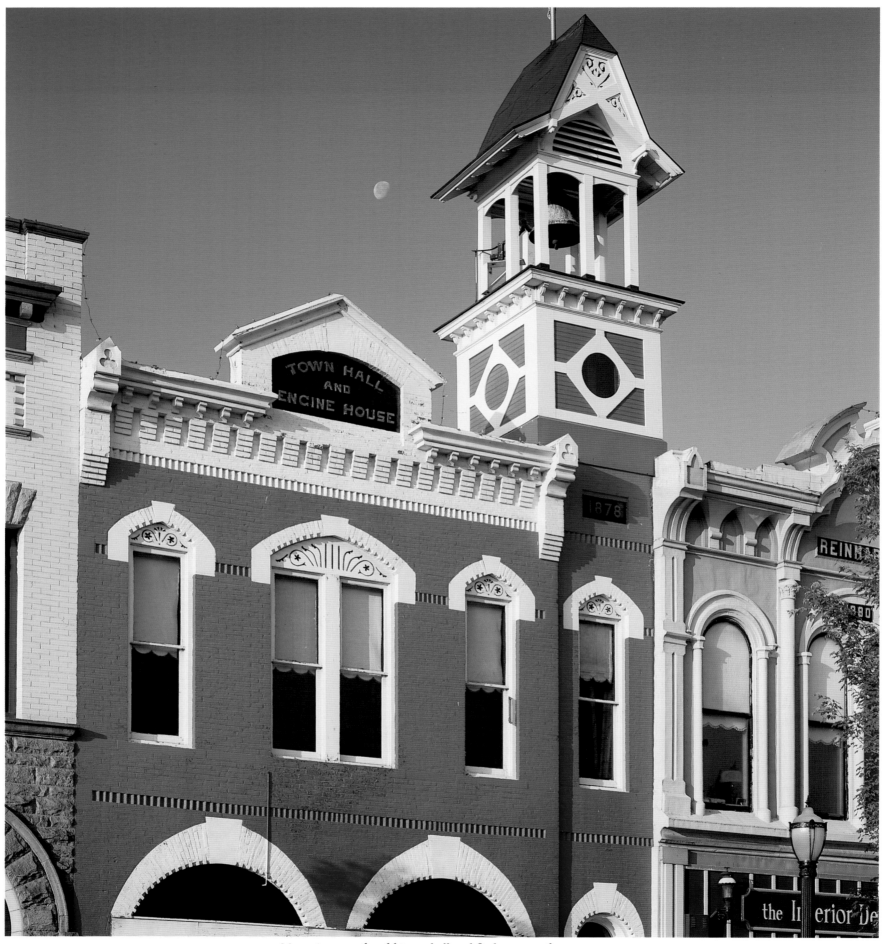

Moonrise over the old town hall and firehouse on the square
in Medina in northern Ohio. After the town's business area suffered major
fires in 1848, 1870, and 1877, the town bought a fire engine which
could be pulled by men or horses and which could pump
425 gallons a minute.

The Trumbull County Courthouse in Warren,
with its copper roof, four statues of justice and four-sided clock tower,
is one of America's finest examples of Richardsonian Romanesque architecture.
It was completed in 1897 and was originally the county seat for all of
Ohio's Western Reserve.

Stan Hywet Hall, the largest private home ever built in Ohio,
was completed in 1915, at a cost of $2 million, for Akron industrialist
Frank Seiberling, founder of The Goodyear Tire & Rubber Company. Stan Hywet
means "stone quarry" in Anglo-Saxon, a reference to the nearby quarry which
supplied the stone used to build the 65-room Tudor Revival mansion.

Looking down Main Street at Zoar, a restored 19th-century
village in Tuscarawas County owned by the Ohio Historical
Society. Zoar was founded in 1817 by 300 German Separatists
fleeing their native land in search of religious freedom.
The community was disbanded in 1898.

A view of the Geauga County Courthouse
from the gazebo on the town square at Chardon in Ohio's
Western Reserve. Chardon is a major center for maple sugaring and
is also in northeastern Ohio's "snow belt," receiving more than
100 inches of the white stuff during many Ohio winters.

9
INTO THE GARDEN

IT WAS a wretched location for a garden, an eroded hillside just above Cincinnati's most polluted creek valley where slaughterhouses made the water run red with pigs' blood and mills showered ash on the neighborhood. The Deer Creek had been called "the Ruhr of the West," and its noted products were machinery, sausage, flour, candles, soap and whiskey, not flowering shrubs and rare trees. But Cornelius Hauck was not put off by the location. When he bought the land along Reading Road in 1924, he dubbed his arboretum-to-be, "Sooty Acres," and took to planting his garden. He said the name was facetious.

Today the name is ironic. "Sooty Acres" has thickened into a wondrous grove, eight acres of rare native and splendid Ohio specimen trees carefully mixed with exotic imports. Beyond the cast iron fence, the worst excesses of the past are gone, the Deer Creek buried under an interstate highway and soft coal burning banished to distant power plants. On Reading Road, the traffic roars away. On this green shady island, only the name reminds you of the restorative powers of the gardening instinct that made or remade this land.

Cornelius Hauck, who died in 1967 after deeding his Sooty Acres to the Cincinnati Park Board, thought the protection and cultivation of groves, gardens and greenspace was "one of the best therapies for the illnesses of our present civilization." He chose these unwanted "Sooty Acres" to demonstrate that healing, explaining, "Today, as never before, the insatiable demands of the automobile and bulldozer daily consume more and more land. The desecration of our inheritance of natural beauty continues apace. We are everywhere going faster to go somewhere else."

No matter where we are going, some naturalists give gardeners short shrift, writing them off as mere prettifiers at best and dangerous meddlers in

The 26-acre Schedel Foundation Arboretum and Gardens is located in Elmore, about 20 miles southeast of Toledo. This lovely estate was the creation and summer home of businessman Joseph Schedel and his wife, Marie. The estate includes a Victorian Mansion, a Japanese garden, and over 300 species of trees and shrubs growing among acres of annuals and perennials.

the natural order at worst. Of course, this view of nature sets the human species apart, not merely "unnatural" but positively "extra-natural." In truth, humans are just another terrestial life form, like oxygen-generating algae or CO_2-belching termites, that have altered the Earth. Our special human nature comes from our consciousness in seeing what we've wrought. In that context, the gardener's view can be one of our finer instincts. It stems from the human predilection to cultivate, mend and simply admire. It puts a totally unrealistic value on the abstract notion that living things have a natural beauty. It's a manmade value but it makes every garden priceless.

In season, Ohio fairly bursts with some of the country's most extravagant expressions of that instinct. There are the great estate gardens such as Stan Hywet near Akron or Kingwood near Mansfield. There are the civic showpieces like the Rockefeller Park greenhouse in Cleveland or the Franklin Park Conservatory in Columbus. There are little-known personal statements like Sooty Acres, easily overlooked in big-city Cincinnati, or the Schoepfle Arboretum, well off the beaten path in the small Lorain County village of Birmingham. There are immense Victorian "garden cemeteries" such as Lakeview in Cleveland and Spring Grove in Cincinnati where marble angels stand eternal guard amidst artfully-planted "natural" landscapes. They are all animated by the human propensity to pick and choose, to plant and wait, to take action and to stand back.

It also shows that humans can take a proper place in nature. At Sooty Acres, Cornelius Hauck struggled for years to establish a specimen of the rare and difficult-to-plant Lea's oak. When he finally got one to take, Hauck called in his attorney and dictated a convenant to the deed, granting the oak tree a lifetime tenancy in Sooty Acres. The Lea's oak is still in residence.

The City of Cleveland Rockefeller Park Greenhouse is located on land given to the city by philanthropist and oil tycoon John D. Rockefeller, the founder of the Standard Oil Company. The outdoor gardens include a talking garden for the blind and a Japanese garden, while the main conservatory houses an orchid room, a tropical house, and a main showhouse with changing seasonal displays.

Zinnias and hundreds of other annuals and perennials can be seen each summer at Kingwood Center, one of Ohio's most spectacular public gardens.

Summer flowers and a picket fence evoke visions of an English cottage garden in a residential suburb of Akron.

Petunias decorate the west terrace at Stan Hywet Hall in Akron, the former estate of rubber industrialist F.A. Seiberling. The 70-acre gardens were designed by landscape architect Warren Manning, who also helped to design Central Park in New York.

Rhododendrons and ferns thrive near Madison in Lake County. The mild lake-effect weather in this part of the Buckeye State is ideal for nurseries and vineyards, which abound in the area.

More than 250,000 tulips and other bulbs flower during
April each year at the Koenig Tulip Farm, located on a wooded
hilltop near Henley in rural Scioto County.

A topiary garden is one of the many attractions at the Otto Schoepfle Arboretum near the scenic Vermilion River at Birmingham in Lorain County. Founder and garden columnist Otto Schoepfle donated the garden to Lorain County Metroparks, which helps to maintain the gardens.

This beautifully maintained herb garden at Kingwood Center is one of more than 40 herb gardens in the Buckeye State. The Herb Society of America has its headquarters at Mentor in Lake County near Holden Arboretum.

Rhododendrons bloom in May near a crypt at Lake View Cemetery in the eastern suburbs of Cleveland. Established in 1869, this 285-acre cemetery and arboretum is the final resting place for many noted Clevelanders, including oil tycoon John D. Rockefeller and President James Garfield.

A coleus forms an abstract pattern at Kingwood Center in Mansfield.

A waterfall cascades into the Japanese Garden at the Schedel Foundation Arboretum and Gardens at Elmore in Ottawa County.

Pansies display a riot of colors in a flower border
at Stan Hywet Hall in Akron. Although the gardens have
changed over the years, the Stan Hywet Hall Board of Trustees
is restoring the gardens to their original design, including a
walled English garden which was designed
in the 1930s by Ellen Shipman.

Charles Bagley rhododendrons are one of hundreds of
varieties of azaleas and rhododendrons in the Helen S. Layer Rhododendron
Garden, part of the Holden Arboretum. Display gardens and a wildflower
garden are nearby, as well as hiking trails through mixed
woodlands and other natural areas.

Gardenview Horticultural Park in Strongsville is a
monument to the dawn-to-dusk, 7-day work weeks lavished on this
16-acre cottage garden and arboretum for more than 40 years by one man,
owner and master gardener Henry Ross. Gardenview has over 10,000 varieties
of plants, including many rarities from around the world.

Kingwood Center in Mansfield is the former estate of Charles King,
a local industrialist. The magnificent gardens, free and open to the public,
dawn to dusk, include huge displays of spring bulbs, an herb garden, several acres
of formal gardens and an orangery containing unusual indoor plants.
The annual and perennial plantings are spectacular
during summer.

These daffodils are part of the lovely 25-acre garden
at Lantern Court, the former estate of Warren and
Maud Corning and now part of the 3,200-acre Holden Arboretum.
For more than 20 years, garden superintendent Tom Yates
has developed and maintained the gardens, where native trees,
shrubs and plants blend with introduced varieties.

Cincinnati is blessed with many fine gardens.
One of the best is the Irwin M. Krohn Conservatory,
located in Eden Park just east of downtown. With
22,000 square feet under glass, the conservatory houses a
tropical house, palm house, orchid house,
and desert garden.

10
THE FOUR SEASONS
AN OHIO PHOTOGRAPHY SUITE

"Anybody can love mountains," a transplant to the Ohio flatlands once remarked. "Spring is so flashy. It takes a certain something to love Ohio in February. It's subtle, like all things of great beauty."

As a climate, Ohio's is beyond excuse. It features summers that baste you in your own sweat, winters that sand the skin off your face, and springs so short and hot or so long and wet that you can't decide between shorts and hip boots. Nobody has a bad word to say about autumns in Ohio. New England may crow about fall color but Ohio is more purely hardwood country. The pines of Maine are evergreen; the maples of Ohio blaze up in a vast firestorm of color.

Autumn crosses Ohio north to south along a gentle gradient of falling temperatures. The wave of red, yellow and orange follows right behind on the calendar, accompanied by the sound of a thousand homecoming bands honking out the alma mater fight song. Whole towns jump to their feet, cheering each fall as local heroes lumber out onto the gridiron. Thankfully, many Ohio farmers still waste their time and ground on pumpkin patches. Cloudy, locally-pressed apple cider reaches even the glossiest city supermarkets.

Spring takes care of itself although transitions come hard to Ohio. Spring can be especially violent. We sit on the climatic curb of Tornado Alley here and listen for the air raid sirens of spring. Yet the worst of this most welcome season is its schedule. Spring comes when it's ready and leaves when it feels like leaving. In Ohio, that can means bare branches into April with the claustrophobic humid embrace of summer arriving a week later. Or spring can deliver a long, fragile string of Camelot days when it only rains at night and the wild flowers hold court from March through July. Then the woods light up with dogwood, wild crabapple and that strangest blossom of spring, the redbud whose buds are not red; the blossoms are. And red is probably the wrong word, as the flowers of the redbud run more toward purple than scarlet. Yet, in the bare woods of early spring, a good stand of redbud throws off a red-purple haze of such startling intensity that it looks almost unnatural.

Winters can be fierce on Little Mountain, part of the Holden Arboretum in Lake County. One of Ohio's only stands of white pine grows here, among the hemlocks and sandstone ledges of this rugged natural area.

But what excuse can be offered for Ohio's two iron-handed seasons? Winter and summer can plead their usefulness. The deep killing frost is a hedge against southern pests such as Kudzu and fire ants. The summer heat that falls from the sky in wet blankets is sucked up by corn, beans, tomatoes and small children. It gives us rich farmland and our youngsters long memories of slow summers.

But only face Ohio's tough seasons straight on. Look out in winter with eyes open. The north wind has a terrible beauty even if it requires a certain sang froid (or a four-wheel drive truck with studded tires) to behold the charm of a snowdrifted country road. Yet, in less-threatening weather, you can escape from the maddening interstate highways. On a bitter, bright day, pull to a stop on a country road, switch off and get out to listen. There's a diamond-hard stillness that comes only in air that feels too cold to move. Because Ohio straddles a climatic fault line, you can also choose your degree of winter—full-blast New England in the north or softly wet and brown in the south. Unfortunately the Ohio winter reserves the right to suddenly turn the geographic tables—a blizzard to the south and a shirt-sleeve afternoon to the north—without a moment's notice.

The Ohio summer is best taken in sips. Our ancestors walked into the Midwest wearing flannel and wool but they soon contrived front porches, awnings, shaded streets and iced drinks. These hot days, we strip off and turn up the air conditioning only to find ourselves brooding by the window, feeling trapped by comfort. Yet you can step out into full summer. Go under the trees. Go along the beds of stubbornly-running streams. Go out into a meadow at sunset and remark on the dozen clear distinctions in light between late afternoon and early evening. Then find the next twelve shades to full night. Chiefly, you must stop fretting about being cooler or drier. Join the ambient temperature and be with the fireflies, the hunting owls and the hallejuah chorus of crickets on a summer's night. Don't fidget in the face of subtle beauty.

A fresh snowfall covers the ground near the Jonathan Hale
Homestead at Hale Farm & Village in the Cuyahoga Valley National Recreation Area.
Other attractions at Hale Farm, which is operated by the Western Reserve
Historical Society, include a sawmill and pioneer craft
demonstrations.

Rows of tulips line the drive to Arthur Koenig's Tulip Farm in the rugged hills of Scioto County near Portsmouth. Nearby is Shawnee State Forest, Ohio's largest contiguous wooded area, as well as a large concentration of Mail Pouch barns along the Ohio River.

A Japanese maple blends with annual and perennial plants in a theme garden at Cincinnati's Ault Park. In late April each year, Ault Park hosts the Cincinnati Flower Show, the largest outdoor horticultural exhibition in the nation.

Daffodils herald spring's arrival along the H. S. Wagner Daffodil Trail in Furnace Run Metropark in Summit County.

Maple trees flower in April along the Olentangy River near
Delaware in central Ohio. These same maples will add to Ohio's
spectacular fall color in mid-October.

May brings a cornucopia of Japanese primroses, azaleas,
and other flowering plants at Lantern Court, part of the Holden Arboretum in
Lake County. Lantern Court also includes a rock garden, a lily pond,
and an English rose garden.

Zinnias and orange spikes of Celosia frame a view of Kingwood Center
in Mansfield. This magnificant estate of the late industrialist Charles K. King
also has a shade garden and a pond with many species of waterfowl.

This rolling hill country near Jelloway in Knox County
is on the fringes of Ohio's Amish country, the world's largest
community of the "plain people."

Sassafras and black oak are common in the sandy
areas of Oak Openings Metropark west of Toledo in Lucas County.
The sand was deposited thousands of years ago by ancient lakes that
covered what is now Michigan. Today, the Oak Openings area is
one of Ohio's richest botanical areas.

A fiery sunset outlines an
old barn in Preble County
near the Indiana border.

Red Maple leaves cover the rocks below Blue Hen Falls
in northeastern Ohio's Cuyahoga Valley National Recreation Area.
A half-mile downstream is another cascade,
Buttermilk Falls.

Snow covers trees and boulders along
the West Branch of the Rocky River in Olmsted
Falls in the western suburbs of Cleveland.

Ice covers Fairport Harbor on Lake Erie in Lake County.
Balmy summer breezes are replaced by frigid arctic winds and "lake effect" blizzards
which often dump more than 100 inches of snow on Lake, Geauga, and
Ashtabula Counties during a hard winter.

Winter snowfalls create a Currier & Ives scene
near Charm in the heart of the world's largest Amish
community in Holmes County.